SHARK'S TOOTH

Also by Marc Elihu Hofstadter

House of Peace (Mother's Hen Press)

Visions (Scarlet Tanager Press)

SHARK'S TOOTH

by Marc Elihu Hofstadter

Regent Press
Oakland, California

Publisher's Cataloging-in-Publication

Hofstadter, Marc Elihu, 1945-
    Shark's tooth / by Marc Elihu Hofstadter.
    p. cm.
    LCCN 2006920648
    ISBN 1-58790-091-2

    1. Gay men--Poetry. 2. HIV-positive men--Poetry.
I. Title.

PS3558.O34S53 2006   813'.6
                          QBI06-600035

Design: Roz Abraham
Cover photo and back cover photo: G. Paul Bishop, Jr.

Manufactured in the U.S.A.
Regent Press
6020-A Adeline Street
Oakland, CA 94608
www.regentpress.net

for David Zurlin

ACKNOWLEDGMENTS

Grateful acknowledgment is made to the editors of the following publications in which these works or earlier versions of them previously appeared:

A & U: America's AIDS Magazine: "Medford, Oregon" (as "Medford, Oregon, 2000")
Bayou: "Mother"
Carquinez Poetry Review: "Portland, Oregon" (as "Visiting Friends")
Cedar Hill Review: "Joe"
Confrontation: "The Game"
Fox Cry Review: "Grayness"
Jeopardy Magazine: "Baseball," "Yule"
Nerve Cowboy: "Arnold Suffin's *Bird in Flight*" (as "Arnold Suffin's Sculpture *Pacem in Terris (Bird in Flight)*")
Off The Rocks: "Autobiography"
Oregon East Magazine: "Raspberries"
Pennsylvania English: "Fluff," "Listening to Artie Shaw"
Phi Kappa Phi Forum: "Mediterraneum Caffe, Berkeley" (as "Mediterraneum Café, Berkeley")
Poet Lore: "The Nap, 1966" (as "The Nap")
RE:AL: "Caravan"
Red Wheelbarrow Literary Magazine: "In the Old City"
The Redwood Coast Review: "The 49 Van Ness Bus," "Captain Jack's Wharf" (as "Jack's Wharf"), "How We Were Alike, Jimmy"

RFD: "The Pencil-Case"
Sanskrit: "Attending a Yeats Play for the First Time"
Soundings East: "Your Name"
Spillway: "Two Young Men" (as "Two Youths")
Swarthmore College Bulletin: "Frank O'Hara's Book
    Jackson Pollock" (as "On Reading Frank O'Hara's
    1959 Book *Jackson Pollock* in 2000")
Whetstone: "Castro and Market" (as "Standing at the
    Intersection of Market and Castro, 1982")
Wisconsin Review: "Love of the Penis"

"Castro and Market" won the Whetstone
    (Barrington Writers Workshop) Poetry Prize for
    2004.

I am particularly grateful to Kim Addonizio, who guided my writing for years, Clive Matson, who taught me expertly and passionately, Sarah Rosenthal, who helped me extend my range, Yves Bonnefoy, who provided me with an admirable model, Marcia Falk, who honed my skills, and Willis Barnstone and Samuel Hynes, who stimulated and encouraged me. I also wish to thank Stephen Kessler, Jannie Dresser, Wendy Breuer, Paul Belz, Dian Gillmar, Leonard J. Cirino, Daniel Marlin, Mitchell Zeftel, David Schooley, Yvonne Cannon, Luis Garcia, Susan Cohen, Christine DeSimone, Peter Kane, and Beverly Burch, fine and helpful writing colleagues. And my friends Firdosh Anklesaria, Donald Caplin, Mayona Engdahl, Jane Falk, Nicholas Follansbee, Gloria, Frédéric, and Claire Grover, Colin Guiver, Les Kong, Sandy Rappy, Donald Sackheim, Mark Sherkow, Peter Straus, and Arnold and Gloria Suffin, for their support. And, not to forget the two who started me writing: David Mus and the late Alfred Levinson. But most of all, David Zurlin, for everything.

CONTENTS

Art Epiphanies

Tribute to James Schuyler, 1923-1991

High-Steppin'

A Brief Study of Beverages 63

Shark's Tooth

ART EPIPHANIES

ART EPIPHANIES

If I listen to an oldies station on my car radio
while crossing the Bay Bridge, it's sure to happen:
the beads my auburn-haired girlfriend and I wore
in Golden Gate Park in '67 sway again in my mind.
If I gaze at a glowing orange-and-purple Rothko
in the San Francisco MOMA,
my whole youth in New York floods back:
white socks and tight black pants, pointless crushes
on straight boys, lonely walks on Broadway.
Picking up *War and Peace* in Cody's Books in Berkeley,
I'm holding it again in a flowering Vermont meadow,
fascinated by lofty, serene clouds above my head
like the ones Prince Andrew watches,
wounded, near death, on the battlefield.
While everything is ending,
art is happening all the time:
old Rolling Stones tunes still hits,
Bly's verse vibrant through snowy fields, war,
surrealism, men's grief, and *ghazals*,
twenty lithe kids shimmying
to Merce Cunningham's limber lines.
Again and again, when the days are passing like rabbits,
my eye remembers the curve of a Rodin bust,
my head reverberates with Stevens' *Death is the mother
of beauty*,
my ears thrill to the Everly Brothers
in their pompadours, wailing *Dream, dream, dream*.

3

POETRY

A sweet release
flows from the pen,
like the rapture of coming,
or an orange oozing its stream of nectar,
or the whoosh when the dam breaks,
and the whole lake
quenches the thirst of the valley.

I learned it from everybody,
and nobody.
Found it, a secret buried in an old book
in a dark basement.

And it sprouted like wild poppies
in my garden.
Each year it blooms more faithfully.
I go outside sometimes at midnight
to find it breathing and glowing in the moonlight,
flourishing while I sleep.

CAPTAIN JACK'S WHARF

One cottage on the wharf blushes like a carnation
in the painting on my wall.
Another imitates the sun's color.
A third's indigo as the early evening Cape Cod sky.
Finally, a tower, red and white,
symbol of the wharf's local fame.
All on top of streaked brown pilings that creak and
snort salt
as waves from England thump against them.
Clouds fluff and roister . . .

My Uncle Sam daubed this work
in Provincetown in the thirties or forties,
before I was born,
when he was younger than I am now,
when, I've heard, his brown eyes and broken nose
conquered all the women,
when he handled the tough kids
in the Bronx high school where he taught,
before he came down with Parkinson's,
before all those shuffling trips
we made from bedroom to bathroom,
before the stroke that made him paranoid.

Sam, you died when I was twenty-seven.
And here I am now,

fifty-seven, in bed, with HIV that pitches me on the
waves
as you were pitched,
my eyes on your gaudy cottages,
your breezy sea,
your pulsing, glittering light.

LOOKING FORWARD
for David

What does it matter that we die?
Everything dies—
poppies, antelope, dinosaurs,
mountain peaks, planetoids, black holes—
even the universe may die.
If everything that is
expires, maybe death itself will be cancelled
and things will reverse themselves—
nebulae and glaciers
and sycamores and crickets
streaming back, grinning,
greeting each other—
"Of course I remember you!"
Maybe the whole thing will go
back to a new Bang
so that my main moment—
the one when I met you—
will be yet to come.

TUESDAY

Azure and hazel gazes glimmer gem-like
as I stroll through delectable morning
Blouses balloon in ragged breeze while
Christmas lights scintillate in sycamores
In a tea bar Darjeeling flowers on my tongue
while my words bounce and rattle like pebbles
down the river of this day
which seems inexhaustible
which carries along
baby carriages, glances, mustaches, hats,
salutations, and movie marquees
Afternoon arrives like a woman in a boa
trailing astonished onlookers
We dally touching the fringes of her skirt
Eventually cities, steeples, and broad plains form
in the underbellies of clouds
Though you may allow rain soon oh day
your subsequent chapters are unknown
and therefore magical to me
You surge like the Pacific in a cove
Ring the air like a carillon
I'm going to stick with you faithfully
Allow me to place my coat
so you may pass gracefully over the gutter

AUTUMN LATE AFTERNOON

My open front door frames a Vermeer.
Eggshell sky with child's-imagination clouds
above terraces of green: pine, magnolia, ivy.
Pale light like the master's suffuses
everything, enters the living room
with a gentle face tired but happy.
Lying on the couch, I'm surrounded
by books, compact discs, furniture
that may last a hundred years, two hundred.
A breeze curls through the doorway.
The hair on my arms rises.
My breathing tingles with the rich
pollen scents that dance in the waning sun.
Soon it'll be dinnertime.
I float like a skiff on a wide sea.

THE GAME

Here I wear green and gold like those around me,
one of thousands pouring into the Coliseum,
and, once the game begins,
can distinguish splitter from slider,
appreciate a popup dropped to get a double play,
notice when the base-runner on first sends up a flair.

My hot dog, garlic fries, and Coke taste like
those I downed with my dad in the Polo Grounds in
the fifties,
at Yankee Stadium as I was growing into a man,
at Briggs Stadium during a summer in Detroit,
that last year before it dawned on me I was gay.

The field's so green, the sunlight so brilliant
the players seem immortals
sporting around, dashing and lunging.
A-Rod is a tall and lithe Achilles,
Barry Zito a wavy-locked Apollo.
A rugged, shaved-headed jock jokes with me
about the bases-loaded walk
that won our A's the game last night.
A frizzy-haired, bespectacled woman
asks me to explain a play.
I scream and high-five with three teenaged boys
whenever the A's score.

I don't want to go home and feel the abyss between
myself
and beefy men screeching down my street in Trans Ams,
women in pants suits meeting in the local coffeehouse
over calculators and cell phones,
businessmen gathering in twos and threes
to talk in low tones on Piedmont Avenue.
I want to stay here.

MY OTHERWISE
(after a poem by Jane Kenyon)

I was born to two loving, depressed people.
It might have been otherwise.
My childhood was half-smiles, half-tears.
It might have been otherwise.
I'm gay, but loved a woman with long, blond hair.
It might have been otherwise.
I wanted to be a teacher, but wound up a poet.
It might have been otherwise.
I have HIV, but have survived many years.
It might have been otherwise.
Everything that's happened to me has its yin and its
yang,
which is to say I've lived in this world.
It might have been otherwise.

IN THE PARK

As I sit on the peeling wooden bench
in a dusty Jerusalem park reading a novel,
at a certain moment my body begins to swell,
my chest puffs out, my head jerks skyward,
my fingers tingle, and my pulse throbs violently.
The trees above me sway, sway, sway in bright light
that penetrates my skull and fills my belly,
I expand, the light takes me over, I lose control,
I'm all light and sky and waving branches
and I wonder, What's going to happen?
when I'm set back down on the bench
that presses against my butt
as though I'm a small craft returned from the high seas
and I stare at the lines of type in the book
till I find my place again.

DUSK

The sky over the dark silhouettes of redwoods,
over campus Greek Revival copper roofs,
over the fairy-tale spires of San Francisco,
over the ocean too low to see,
is salmon and vermilion.
Four or five people read in the café.
No one speaks.
On the white gazebo a string of yellow lights
switches on automatically,
as though they decided it was time.
It's too dark for day, too light for night,
moment when the minutes almost stop
and something hovers in the air.
Death come softly?
The heart too full to articulate its love?
Time catching its breath?
The hush deepens,
a dog barks far off,
and the moon rises in the east over the Berkeley hills,
huge and yellow.
Is it trying to tell me something?
I can't quite understand,
but as I walk home to cook dinner,
each face, each streetlight, my own visible breath,
seems softer than usual.

LEONARDO'S GRAVE AT AMBOISE

You're under the plain yellow stone
in the tiny chapel's floor,
which I reach out and touch.
You lived long, for your time—
sixty-seven years. Now you're a name,
a few world-revered paintings,
and this stone.
You're ordinary
as a blue patch of sky above the Loire.
You're part of the earth, whose tiny stones
and inconspicuous wildflowers
you depicted with such dexterity.
Even if I imagine you pacing
the narrow second-floor walkway
of your home Clos-Lucé up the road,
your thoughts are nothing but
a whispering breeze.
I want to talk with you,
Leonardo, whom I loved as a boy
when I saw your drawings of men
and thought you must be like me,
when I read your plans
for submarines and skyscrapers.
I have lots of questions for you,
there's so much I could learn,
but you're dumb, not a trace!

The light filters through glass
onto your stone.
I speak a few words
but you don't respond.
I think you'll be still here forever.

MOTHER

Watching the couple wheel the blear-eyed,
twig-limbed mother of one of them into the tea bar,
ply her with First Flush Darjeeling and double-mocha
torte,
their whole attention fixed on making her happy for
one hour,
while she shows little sign of noticing much of
anything,
whether cake, or tea bar, or them,
I think of my mother—
how she couldn't enjoy any restaurant meal but pot
roast,
how there were long silences in our conversations,
how she'd complain about needing to wear diapers,
and how she'd cry when thanking me ("all she had in
the world")
when I drove her back to the assisted care facility.
Looking at this woman laboriously chew and swallow,
I wonder if I'll feel sorry for myself when I'm old,
if I'll look squinty and out of it as she does,
if I'll still write poems.
Easy to think one won't be like that,
and Artur Rubenstein's playing at ninety-six
may have been the best of his career,
but aren't I likely to give up?
Suddenly I want to feed the woman chunks of pastry,

assure her she's doing as well as anyone.
But they're wheeling her out,
and the tea bar's still as a Monday church.

OLD WOMAN

She comes into view through the tea bar's window
gradually—shoulders straight, back slightly hunched,
gnarled hands firmly placing the walker's stiff cage
a step ahead, a step ahead.
Tiny, thin-boned, no larger than a bittern or heron,
she wears a little girl's flowered dress,
and her cheeks are pudgy and white as a doll's,
her hair a mass of wispy curls.
She sports big, pink glasses and a hint of a smile.
Where is she headed?
How far has she been walking?
It seems she can't take another step,
but she does.
I'd like to ask her how she finds the strength
to continue walking, to proceed alone,
while I sit here complaining to my friends.
I'm twenty-five or thirty years younger than she is,
afraid I'm going to die of AIDS.
If she'd look at me, maybe I'd absorb some of her
courage.
Do her eyes gleam at me for a moment?
I step onto the sidewalk and watch her progress
down the avenue, step after methodical step,
ten minutes, twenty.
Then she's a mere dot against gray pavement.

YOUR NAME

When you slipped into the jam-packed coffeehouse
ten minutes after I'd started my reading,
I knew I was done for.
Your hazelnut-eyed, downy face,
nose worthy of a Roman,
mouth moist as a peach,
skin like a poplar's smooth bark ...
I continued reading somehow,
but kept shuffling my papers,
and my mouth turned dry.
Your eyes shone;
you scribbled notes and laughed at my jokes.
Each laugh brought me closer to,
I don't know,
falling to my knees.
I loved the way your gaze narrowed
in seriousness.
When you came up to buy my book,
I gave it to you free;
you asked me to inscribe it,
and so I learned your name
just before you walked out the door,
with me almost following.
And I held that name in my mind
like a keepsake,
one short word,
poetry.

GLOWING CATS

You sauntered into my poetry reading,
nut-brown eyes darkening,
pen soon scribbling notes,
long eyelashes (I'll be honest) making my penis rise.
But what got me was how I felt for a month after,
two months, three,
how my whole being kept lifting
at each thought of your face raised like a deer's,
your smile like an arc of poppies,
your sandy voice
(and I know some of it is ego,
and some of it lust).
After that, each attentive set of eyes,
every rush of applause,
seemed an echo, a reminder.
Elms, buses, cats started to glow from inside.
It doesn't really matter that I'll never see you again,
that you're tooling around Berkeley with other people,
girls, maybe,
not thinking of me.
It's likely we wouldn't have had much to say to each other.
You're a boy; I'm an old fart.
But that evening was like sun on twilight birches,
or whoosh of the undertow as it falls back into the surf,
or voice of the beloved whispering the same words over
and over:
it is I, it is I.

TWO YOUNG MEN

I like to think myself reasonable,
so it makes no sense that I'm preoccupied
by two tawny, jet-haired, noble-nosed young men
who burst into the summer tea bar
and stride like roan stallions to the counter.
One tosses the hair out of brash eyes.
As they speak and laugh,
their teeth flash like whitecaps.
I know looks don't mean intelligence or decency,
I realize their flesh will wither
by the time they're old as I,
and I'm happily married to a man,
but, damn it, try as I might
to concentrate on Galway Kinnell's
Imperfect Thirst, I can't think of anything
but their cocoa eyes, pliant bodies,
and moist, vermilion lips.
The fact of there being two puts an exclamation
on it, as if God were saying, "See,
I can make as many as I want!"
For me it seems like overkill, and indeed just
the thought of putting my hands on their curls
nearly does me in. I'd love to hear their voices
(they sit on the other side of the room),
which resemble purling brooks no doubt,
but will meet these two only in some better life,

one in which cats learn to caress mice,
or rapture rains from the skies.
I while away the minutes, aware of their presence
as I am of the muggy air and bronzed light,
until I completely give up and simply bask
in the incandescence of these two
who make my logic and wisdom ridiculous.

LOVE OF THE PENIS

What's more ridiculous than love of the penis,
that one-eyed mushroom that sprouts from a dank
thicket
and rises higher and higher, like some witless lord in
his castle
whose pride exceeds that of his king?
Nothing could be sillier than its mindless push,
which has no thought of ideas, heartache, or baseball,
which glows when petted, like a mawkish kitten,
and resembles a worm slithering through slimy loam.
Its emptiness is like that of the moon,
or snow, or a mental block.
What is it we men are so proud of?
Yet the penis serves a few purposes:
it teaches a man to enjoy his body,
as a fire engine entertains a mass of kids;
it fosters friendship,
like a funny-looking guy always panting for fans;
and it purges the mind of muck,
like Zen meditation,
clearing away beach memories and to-do lists,
focusing the attention on the moment,
until a man's nothing but pure flow,
Buddhist definition of reality.

RASPBERRIES

The ones I glimpsed from the bus this morning
looked so succulent among the piled-up peaches and
plums.
Crushing them on my tongue, I thought,
would be like owning a château in the Côte-d'Or
and sipping *Savigny-les-Beaune* with my veal roast,
or poring over intricate letterings by Tacitus, Anselm,
and the Venerable Bede in cavernous libraries,
or viewing bardos of clear light and great compassion
in a mud temple high above Lhasa.

I thought and thought of them all day,
imagined touching their moist,
faceted bowls with my fingers,
popping them like prizes into my mouth,
and believed I couldn't be happy without them.
They hovered, glistening,
above my in-box, computer screen, and conference
table.

So after work I took the same bus, got off,
and went to buy my tantalizing dreams,
but as I examined them up close
I saw there were black spots all over them,
and many were small and overripe.

RUBY KING CHINESE BAKERY

They gulp tea and down sweets at pink Formica tables.
Clad in worn plaid shirts and faded baseball caps,
they may have been street repairmen,
cab drivers, shop owners.
Their leathery faces, seen-it-all looks,
and loud banter take me in
like a basin full of warm water.

I imagine they're discussing
why Li Po drowned in the Yellow River,
or how the Tao, "being great ... flows ...
and having gone far ... returns."
They're probably debating one-size-fits-all wrenches,
assessing the COLA on their Social Security,
or joking about Metamucil.
It makes no difference.
Their up-and-down cadences echo
four thousand years of history,
a legacy some poor Yankee like me
can never hope to inherit.

I observe their gray temples,
brisk commands,
the way they lift spongy pastries
with gnarled fingers.
I sit hour after hour,

drinking sweet, milky tea,
letting waves of speech wash over me,
being near these men
who are not my tribe,
who are neither my relatives nor my friends,
who breathe the air of China
here in downtown Oakland.

ALEXANDER CALDER'S STABILE ON THE LAWN OF THE UNIVERSITY ART MUSEUM, BERKELEY

The huge, black iron bird—
plate, bolt, and hinge—
curves his wings free
in a flight that will never
take place in this air,
that is always occurring
in another world we can't see
where bonsai trees grow huge
and fish kiss in depths.
I touch and test
the stiff instruments of flight,
but he doesn't notice.
He's been soaring a long time
over peaks, plains, seas.
The Babylonians saw him
and drew his wings on beasts.
The Greeks worshiped him.
Michelangelo made him an angel
to guard over mankind.
Now he swoops low
over the fresh-mown grass,
unhurried,
not a word or smile.
He's too busy with the

apparatus of freedom.
There's no explaining to him
desire's limits,
the argument for caution.
He'll fly until the sun goes down,
and then eclipse the moon.

TO THE FRENCH LANGUAGE

You were foreign as the names Meaulnes and
Desqueroux,
yet came nearer with a homely *Larousse* or *Robert*.
Though you gave me many embarrassing moments in
class,
I eventually learned how to cater to your whims.
I savored your *madeleines* with breakfast tea,
imagined walking with you down poplared lanes
that led to ruined castles and Alpine villas.
I began to dream of you.
Soon I decided you were everything I sought,
so I joined you for a year at *13 rue du Grenier à Sel,
Orléans*.
There you spoke through fruit vendors, lamp salesmen,
movie clerks.
You were even on television!
We traded prepositions, *oh là-là's, n'est-ce pas's*:
it was like singing all day long.
I showered you with compliments, which you took as
your due,
for you're nothing if not proud.
I knew I'd lose you, which added to your charm.
When we parted I realized I'd never have you like that
again.
Now I hear you in snatches on radio broadcasts from
the U.N.,

tossed back and forth on university campuses,
issuing from the open doors of arthouses.

And when I declaim du Bellay to the elms,
I recognize your voice in the leaves' excited rustling.

TO A FRIEND

Put on the noseband and inhale the rye;
the bug's got you and you know why.
One pull on the rope, you're going to die.

Now that you're ill you can see clear.
It takes acumen to be queer
in this land where men can only slug a beer.

Thin and frail, you're star-like,
but your body's ridiculous as a little kike
racing for dollars on a souped-up bike.

Con moto, now: enter the pylon
of the great temple, get a smile on,
cover your legs with the silkiest nylon.

There's no blight where the haddock goes,
the civet, the tapir, and the duck's webbed toes.
There is where the immortal flows.

THE 49 VAN NESS BUS

The 49 Van Ness bus feels heavy as a freighter,
with its drunk slurring "How ya doin', man?,"
its old woman in torn cotton dress
carrying a plastic bag crammed with empty soda cans,
its youth, headphones throbbing rap,
who stares angrily at me,
two teenage girls with pancake makeup,
long blue nails, and hard, emerald eyes.

How can it roll smoothly on?
Shouldn't the driver set the motor idling and
announce,
"This coach is carrying too much sorrow to proceed"?
Then I would fulfill my latent vocation:
take all these unshaven, pockmarked, and powdered
faces in my hands,
assure them I love them,
that this bus will take them home.

The coach lurches to a stop,
and it occurs to me I might get my chance,
but a fight has broken out
between two boys in soiled sweatshirts
and the driver's calling Central.
The bus seems too leaden to move
but, after two thickset cops remove the kicking

offenders,
it does.
Nothing can stop it.

TRIBUTE TO JAMES SCHUYLER,
1923-1991

WORDS

I would have liked
to know
you. Easy
to imagine
planting all
sorts of roses
together,
splashing on Taylor's
Eau de Portugal,
quarreling, making
up. Up
into the blue
we would have soared.
True? You were
so smart, a wit.
Could I have
kept up?
And you were short,
chubby,
not my type.
Would I
have been yours?
Maybe just say
we'd be friends …
but at that thought of daily
reality, fantasy

fades: friend,
we never met.
We're worlds apart,
I'm just reading
your book
years after you died.
I hold your
page, turn it,
stroke your broad
cover—together with you
in quiet. You
wrote tender words.
I write mine,
send them up
into the sky.

LISTENING TO ARTIE SHAW

These old bones creak
but listening to you, Artie,
this evening,
I find I'm dancing
along the hall to my bedroom—
swinging! Davey
likes me to dance
in front of him
when we're by ourselves
and laughs, eyes shining—
as though I were good!
I've really only
danced sixties rock 'n' roll,
never even heard you
or Woody or Glenn or Tommy
before now, in this
final year of the millennium.
My parents might have
listened to this
sixty years ago,
sung and danced!
That's a funny thought,
as I am now,
rotund,
swinging down the hallway
teenager-like.

My parents are long dead,
my knees and legs ache,
it's dark out,
but I'm dancing,
dancing, dancing
to the end of the night.

THE PENCIL-CASE

makes me think of Orléans.
I'll never know which
of my students it belonged to
(brown leather, gold zipper
down the middle, neat
rectangular steel rod
inside for paperweight)—
. Pierre the cute, who I
had such a crush on, Patrick
the sharp-nosed, smart, dangerous,
or what-was-his-name (it's been
twenty-five years) with the shabby
work jacket and jeans? The
classroom was large, in a barracks-
like prefab building, the seats
low behind small wood desks.
The profusion of ochre poplars
and pink roses of Orléans' autumn
wrapped us in its cocoon.
The light, as usual,
was gray and muted. I just
went over to the desk
after class, attracted by
the leather's sheen,
and pilfered it,
and whoever owned it doesn't know

even now it was me.
Ah pencil-case,
where is Pierre now?
Orléans?
Am I absolved
after all this time?

FLUFF

It's been
brief.
I've felt
snow bite
on a French
morning, read
most of Dostoyevsky's
novels, known
days of bliss kissing
a beautiful man. What
am I
left? Dizzi-
ness, weak
legs and arms,
this feeling
of being
fluff
easily blown away. What
comforts me,
icily,
is the vastness of
space, how small
everything
is.
I stretch
my arm out

toward a star
six thousand
light-years away
where things have
been going on
almost forever.

HOW WE WERE ALIKE, JIMMY

Why do I feel I
knew you? For starters,
we both loved Brahms'
Second Piano Concerto.
Forsythia.
Getting away to
Vermont. Sleeping on
cool sheets.
We were nostalgic for
days of sweaty sun
in Florence—
some of our better years.
Then there were the other
times; I've survived years of
illness and madness,
as you did—
nights alone, sleepless,
popping tranks,
repeating lines
from loved poems—you on
Long Island, me in
Santa Cruz, where I
didn't yet know
your name. If I
had, I could have dashed
off letters professing

our affinity,
but you were famous,
me a kid who
didn't even admit
to being gay—
would it have come
to anything?
We were both born in
November, and shared
a Scorpio's suffering
and passion.
You loved and loved and loved
and lost. I've won,
so far, and must
admit I like growing old
better than you did,
alone there in the Chelsea,
chugging coffee, smoking,
trying not to drink,
waiting and waiting to go
for a haircut, or to John's,
or for flowers . . .
until Tom came into your life,
that is.
Tom's *blond hair/diamond-*
dusted with raindrop fragments—
we both loved men
and beauty.

The beauty of
veined leaves
and all the ways
you described the sky,
light, and shade,
and how shadows—
loneliness, depression, death—
gradually encroached
and cast their spell
over you,
as they will me,
one way or another,
some day.
We both had Olivettis,
liked dogs,
caught fireflies
as kids, you in
West Virginia, me in
Westchester. Mr.
Schuyler, James,
Jimmy, what
do I want
to say? You lived and
died. I live
now and read your poems.
Quiet as you were
and modest,
you lit the way.

Rest now forever
blessed tired heart,
wakening otherwhere
in bell-like blue.

HIGH-STEPPIN'

MOTOR CITY

I was washing the car when the carburetor went boing and I knew I didn't know enough about winter. Hattie had left three times and I ended the month with a migraine. Well, I was putting the soap away when Julie came up to me and said, How'd you like to dance? I said, If you're for real I'll follow along. Then the cold hit, and you know I'm no good at high-steppin', so I just shut the front door and put the stereo on. It played *Here You Are in Old Detroit*, my favorite song. I jumped and swung, just like old times. Finally the announcer came on and said, You're done, Sam. So I stopped.

YULE

What I love about Christmas is how nothing works.
Our tree scratches the ceiling, presents get switched,
Santa's delayed on the I-5. One year there was a power
outage. There was a great silence until someone had the
idea, let's tell stories. One told the one about his uncle
and the fish, a second spun the tale of thirteen Albanian
car mechanics, and I chimed in with the whole long
narrative of my unmarried adult sibling, neither my
brother nor my sister, a creature of great charm and no
little talent. By the time I'd finished, the juice was on
again, we sang carols, and someone brought in spiced
cider, but nothing was quite the same.

JOE

There was a fellow named Joe who wasn't the marrying kind. He had four guns and a grandfather clock and a house full of crates. He'd fill the crates with stuff—flags, cell phones, porno magazines—and carry them from room to room. When he was satisfied with the way they looked, he'd lean back in his Naugahyde recliner and chug a beer. He lived on a plain street in a plain suburb, and minded his own business. Sometimes he mowed his lawn, or changed his truck's oil in the driveway, and then laid dandelions out over the stain. But last January Joe got fed up. He went outside in his underwear—it was snowing—and shined his flashlight into his neighbors' windows. One called the police and Joe was sentenced to prison for seven years. He keeps busy there, carrying crates from office to office, making himself useful.

BASEBALL

It's my pastime. I even played it in France, where the "ball" is square and you hit it with a mop. Baseball's eternal, like the moon, or Beethoven, or remorse. I never learned to hit properly but I take a big swing and try not to whiff. My hero F.D.R. couldn't play it, of course, but he liked to listen on the radio with the sound way up. I like to think I listened with him. I find F.D.R. sexy with his wheelchair and all. I dream he's patrolling center field like Tommy Tresh, making over-the-shoulder grabs. But he and I weren't destined for each other. Besides, he couldn't hit the curve ball.

L.A.

is the kind of place where you stroll around for a few hours and everyone starts to look the same. I saw a muscular guy in a mauve tank top on La Cienega who started multiplying like the stars people see when they get knocked out in comic books. Three hundred elderly Jewish women passed me on the street holding a bag of leftovers. I hoped one of them would turn out to be my deceased grandmother. Then there are the Latino boys. Do all of them blink their long black eyelashes? Do they all sprout coppery down on their forearms? The sun bathes everyone the same in L.A. In December last year it actually rained, and buildings, benches, and taxis looked like a bunch of wet cardboard cutouts. Downtown needs sun to produce smog, juice bars require it to make people thirsty, streets use it to reflect off sunglasses. Everyone wears sunglasses. They create a second world in their glassy depths.

CARAVAN

"To be Jewish is to suffer." You could interpret the works of Heine, Kafka, and Singer this way. A rabbi keened minor-chord Hebrew melodies over the fresh grave. Chocolate-crumbly dirt was heaped by its side. Three *zaftig* matrons held hands and danced, breasts falling out of their blouses. "I've never seen such a thing!" exclaimed the mother, slapping her sides with a whip. I dreamed an interminable caravan of creaky wagons laden with carpets, dates, Bibles. It wound through a desert to a palm-ringed oasis. There, across the turquoise water, a group of Arabs and Jews faced each other, raised their muskets, and fired.

GREEN BOWL

I'd bang the bronze lion's-head knocker three times against the heavy, maroon, metal door. My Aunt Eve would open it, I'd bound inside, jump into the lap of my Nanny, and cover her wrinkled face with kisses. Her skin smelled pungent, like rotting fruit or a drawer of old handkerchiefs, and became even more fragrant with my saliva. She'd laugh and call me her *bubbula*. This word, which I later learned, to my surprise, meant "little grandmother," and which I discovered Jewish grandmothers often call their grandchildren, was the only word Nanny could say. She'd forgotten all the rest, whether in her native Russian, Yiddish, or English. She was *old*, I knew, and this was part of her definition for me: old, senile, grandmother. She'd laugh as I kissed her, and I'd laugh, too. "Nanny, Nanny!" I'd exclaim, and she'd shout *"Bubbula, bubbula!"*

Then the moment would come. Nanny would raise her gnarled right index finger and point at the bowl resting on the round, blond table halfway across the living room. I'd rush over to it, take the lid off, and see what lay within. Round, white balls of peppermint, spiraled with red; or rectangular chocolate biscuits imprinted, each identically, with a word I couldn't read; or red, green, yellow, and purple Chuckles with a sugary surface and smooth, slick insides that would hold the imprint of my teeth. I'd pick up a few and run back to Nanny's lap. She'd laugh and call me her *"bubbula"* again. I'd stay in her lap awhile, biting into my cookie or chocolate, and feel her body shake as we laughed.

I don't know what happened to the green bowl. For a while my parents kept it, though at some point the cover mysteriously disappeared. Then the whole thing was gone.

GRAYNESS

Dirty pearls of rain drip off the eaves of this tea bar, with its picture windows, peach-colored upholstered armchairs, and rubber plants. Today my lover will have a CAT scan. It wasn't raining when his illness began. Leaves were turning auburn and henna, and we kicked our way through them on a walk to the Rose Garden, where we examined the late fall varieties. During our many years together, we've walked the jammed streets of New York City, ancient alleys in Paris, Tilden Park's bright, grassy trails. This morning I told him, I'll be thinking of you when you have the test, at 3:00. That's now. The rain streams in beady rivulets down the window, cold seeps through my clothes, the stereo repeats a hypnotic refrain. I try to absorb the drops, but they slip away and get lost in wide, slick sheets that run out into the glittering street.

A BRIEF STUDY OF BEVERAGES

in memory of Kenneth Koch

I like to drink tea,
though it can give you irritable bowel syndrome or
dyspepsia.
I love the word "dyspepsia."
SFTGFOP tea is Super-Fine Tippy Golden Flowery
Orange Pekoe,
which is actually pronounced "Peck-oh,"
as in "peckerhead,"
a name I have been called more than once.
Tea comes from the *Camellia sinensis* bush,
which is in the *Camellia* family that produces
those compact, flat, pink or white blossoms
and thereby is not only useful but beautiful.
In non-English-speaking countries
herbal tea is not considered tea,
so when someone offers you a rose hips blend as tea
you may wish to snobbishly refuse it,
saying you only drink the real thing.
Sleepytime's an herbal concoction
blended by a company founded by hippies
in the sixties, then taken over
by a large corporation;
I don't mention names for legal reasons,
and touch lightly on the topic
of corporate cultural domination in our country,
about which a whole additional poem could be
written.

Coca-Cola's not a health-oriented beverage
but the whole world's fallen in love with it,
and drinks it as though it were necessary
for the continuation of life—
as it actually is for a good portion of the American
economy.
Dr. Pepper isn't prescribed by doctors,
and is really *Coke* in disguise.
Nehi was my favorite orange drink
when I was knee-high to a grasshopper,
but has been driven out of business by *Orangina*,
whose French name and provenance
render it the preference of yuppies and artistes
everywhere.
Red Bull gives you wings . . .
and three nights of insomnia.
Fizzy water is called many things:
club soda, spritzer, tonic water, seltzer,
mineral water, *eau gazeuse*, and so on.
My parents as children had it mixed at drugstore
counters
with popular "tonics" thought good for health;
"organic" food and "mineral supplements"
may seem equally quaint to our children's children.
Margaritas stimulate both the salt industry
and the Mexican economy,
so getting drunk on them is an altruistic act.

There are many drinks with wonderful names—
Cointreau, Dalwhinnie, *pitú, marc* (my favorite)—
but surface loveliness doesn't always go along with taste;
for example, the exquisitely-named *Fernet-Branca*
has the savor of bitter licorice.
There's a theory about flavored beverages:
they were invented when a peach
fell and dissolved into a stream
whose waters drifted into the mouth
of a skinny-dipping cave woman.
How discovery comes to us at unexpected moments!
You must beware of some drinks, like prune juice;
the sweeter it is,
the faster it will make you run for your life.
Shall we consider barium a drink?
It comes in jars and glasses,
and the nurse tries to encourage you, smiling,
assuring you it tastes like malted milk.
What indeed makes for "drink-ness"?
The philosophers haven't weighed in sufficiently on
the subject.
Cognac tasted by experts
that is swirled around the mouth, then spit out?
Orange-flavored *Metamucil?*
Robitussin?

Then there's the world of wine,
so multifarious I leave it to the many experts

far more qualified than I to explain it.
Suffice it to say there's no more delightful way
to have a really good time,
to become what they call *bosco absoluto*,
than to analyze and evaluate
several interesting vintages with colleagues.
There's milk, which starts us out sucking on breasts,
and then leaves us gasping all our lives for more.
Let's not forget about *Ovaltine*,
which I've heard advertised for fifty years,
and which no one,
to my knowledge,
has ever tasted.
Or about port, which,
if you drink a lot of it,
will make you very mellow
until you come down with the gout.

Finally, there's water,
essential beverage, basis of life,
drink we imbibe from the tap,
take pills with,
and swallow accidentally while swimming,
that we consider precious when not enough of it falls
from the sky
(it's the only beverage I know of that falls from the sky),
and that wild boars and hyacinths drink as greedily as
we.

Where would we be without beverages?
Without H2O to wash down our curry,
cold duck to put us in a good mood,
wine to sip when we're nervous about a date
with that girl down the block
with the blond stubble on her legs?
The argument could be made that they're
the foundation of civilization, a fluid base
of orangeade, ale, and applejack.
How unstable are the works of man;
how varied and ever-changing the world of beverages!
Perhaps we should worship them:
all-powerful *Absolut*, merciful Zinfandel,
bountiful bourbon, regal *Corona*,
generous *Bristol Cream*!

SHARK'S TOOTH

SHARK'S TOOTH

accompanies me everywhere.
Down boutiqued streets.
At the ballpark.
It glistens in sea spume.
Flowers can't soften its edges.
Rain won't wash it away.
At dawn it bathes with me,
slips under the covers in the dark.
Every attempt to negotiate a truce with it fails.
One day it will bite through to the bone.

AUTOBIOGRAPHY

At seven I was a good little boy
except for meeting my buddy Larry once a month for
sex.
In fourth grade Miss Babbitt chose me as her pet,
and made the kids listen to my two-hour talk on birds.
After I made out with Lyra in the movie theater's back
row,
I told my parents,
and their screaming ensured I'd be a monk for years.

My father read Nietzsche and pondered Truth
while my mother taught kids *"Für Elise"* on the piano.
I lusted after boys and John F. Kennedy,
but spent all my time turning dry pages:
Dostoyevsky, Faulkner, Stendhal.
I thought I'd write the Great American Novel.
My parents took me to an acne doctor in New York
City.

Then I moved to California
just in time for the Summer of Love.
I wore beads and tie-dyes,
swooned before the Velvet Underground at the Fillmore.
Ann seduced me over wine and roast lamb,
and I rose up a man, then collapsed
in a cloud of marijuana smoke and voices in my head.

Lisa helped me put things back together.
By Thousand Islands Lake we fucked in swirling
starlight.
After she left me I listened to James Taylor's
"Fire and Rain" a thousand times.
In grad school Bill and I would enter a bookstore,
fill our arms with novels, and walk out, right past the
clerk.
I later sold my pilfered *War and Peace* for peanuts.

My wife and I gathered wildflowers by the Loire
near our apartment in Orléans.
I filled my string bag each day with meat, mushrooms,
wine
before preparing *escalopes de veau* or *boeuf braisé*.
In Israel I haggled with merchants in the Old City
as dust motes hovered in shafts of dim light.
Once a man in a *kefiyah* chased me from a cemetery I
was exploring.

Back in the U.S. I came out, discovered I was positive,
then fell sick with a disease
too exotic for you to recognize.
I walked to a duck pond and through fields
of poppies and lupine until I was better.
I wrote poetry about death, then met a man with wavy
hair

who made me leap inside.

I catalogue books now and answer reference questions,
take pills every eight hours that keep me alive,
walk around Lake Merritt on sunlit afternoons,
and at night gaze at the stars,
astonished at their ancient light.

GYPSY GIRL

In a sepia photo in an antique album
a young girl leans confidently against a fence.
Her hair falls in gypsy curls,
her eyes are bright with daring,
and she wears a loose-fitting, white peasant blouse,
while a charm dangles jauntily from her neck.

My mother!

My mother, who cleaned the house dull-eyed,
replied to people's interest with a rueful smile,
and sat in dark rooms reading Dad's books.
My kind, sad mother.

So there were two:
the young girl who played jacks with her sister Evelyn,
raced around the block,
dared and double-dared to flirt with the young iceman;
who double-dated with her friend Frieda,
played piano four hands,
their fingers bumping when the going got rough;
whom Dad held by the waist
as they danced to Glenn Miller and Artie Shaw,
kissed;
whom he called,
in a letter I once saw,

"my angel" . . .

and my mother,
who raised me thinking the world dark and sad.

Two women.
I weigh them, each in a palm of my hands.

I try to add them up, but they still make two.
This isn't arithmetic, this is life.

Two women.

I gaze at this laughing, brassy girl.

Who was my mother?

HEADING HOME

Driving home from the city at night
in our canary yellow 1955 Mercury
I said "Mom, Dad, I'm scared"—
I didn't know why—
so Dad stopped the car at a pull-out,
you moved to the back seat that smelled of vinyl and,
as Dad started the motor up again,
I put my head in your soft lap.
Lying there,
looking into the darkness through the side window,
I knew every curve in the highway
and could picture just what I'd see if it were light:
the big peaked-roof hotel in Yonkers,
the crumbling red-brick toy factory in Pelham,
New Rochelle's stand of tall cottonwoods.
I looked up into your hazel eyes
and through your black hair falling all around me,
smelled the perfume of your body,
and felt your smile take me in.
That car still moves in the darkness
as the trees go whizzing by
and we head home.

DAD

Your great bald head and big belly made you
God to me, as did your aim to know
everything. Your Chesterfield-fogged
study was stacked with Aristotle,
Nietzsche, Wordsworth, Bibles,
George Gamow, microbiology textbooks,
Morris' Logic, law tomes, Gibbons,
Differential Calculus, How to Plant a Garden.
I'm sure you read Faust too, yet amassed
facts, hypotheses, wisdoms like a fat black spider
weaving a world-spanning web.
How did I feel having God for a father?
Small as a flea, awed, proud.
But what could I ever be?
When you rocked me in your arms,
crooning "Aaah, aaah, bay-bee," I believed,
I believed in God.

But there comes a time for gods to die.
Since thought was enshrined in your temple,
I thrust my blade there,
planting feeling's banner atop your contemplating
globe.
But you didn't die.
We fought like brothers.
You set up Hegel, Adam Smith, Nixon.

I countered with Freud, fucking, poetry.
While you taught classes on *Being and Time*
I smoked grass, slept around, wrote verse.

When I started to hear the voice
of the "Black Angel of Death,"
you lectured the psychiatrists,
blamed flower children,
denounced McGovern.

When I came out, you said your heart was broken.
Men were not meant to love one another.
Meanwhile your books failed to bring renown.
You visited Heidegger in Freiburg
and he served you tea and cookies,
but he was master and you, disciple.

You died in your recliner
in the middle of the night.
In the mortuary I held your right big toe,
cold and clayey, in my hand.
Then, at the cemetery,
as the rabbi keened piercing Hebrew songs,
as we all cried for someone absent,
you went underground in me.
Now I battle with you inside my belly.
You smile, cry, rage, pout,
demand as much attention as ever.

You've become again the infant neglected by his parents
that you were thirty-five years before my birth.
I'm fed up,
but I nurture you
and we march in lockstep like cousins,
like two people who have known each other
a thousand years,
two men yoked together for the duration.

BIRDING

"Cedar waxwing!" cried my buddy Petey,
pointing to the north, and sure enough, there
one solitary of the species I loved most
curled tiny black toes around a spindly branch,
its creamy chest focusing the pre-dawn light.
Nine-year-old campers, we aimed our binoculars
and almost dropped our field guides
as an indigo bunting hopped across the stubbly field.
Warren, our counselor, whispered "Quiet, guys!"
when Everett and Chip started to horse around.
Then a rose-breasted grosbeak cleaved the dark sky in
two
as first yellow began to burn on the horizon.
Ruffed grouse, nuthatch, scarlet tanager, bobolink,
titmouse, Baltimore oriole, brown thrasher,
meadowlark:
so many saints flapping saffron, cobalt, ochre,
vermilion wings while cheeping mystical
tick-tick-tick's, chick-a-dee-dee-dee's, and chir-r-up's,
the gleaming icons in our kids'-eye,
dewy temple of scratchy bushes, pungent sage and
thyme,
steaming reeds, and bronzed deer turds.
Oh, to wake again at five A.M.,
pull on chinos and baseball jersey and dash to the fields
where the flickers, juncos, and kingbirds are fluttering
in air just beginning to turn humid!

FRANK O'HARA'S BOOK
JACKSON POLLOCK

When I first thumbed these pages, Frank,
your flesh was live and could quiver.
1959.
Having taken the New Haven local to Manhattan
to taste the riotous Pollocks at the Modern,
I bought your book in the museum store,
not knowing you were a poet.
I was a kid—fourteen to your thirty-three.
I wonder if I ever saw your broken nose in the lobby.
If our eyes met.
You were the blade's edge, Frank,
laughter in the street.
Now, I caress your pages forty-five years later
and it's a little like touching you.
A gap of years still separates us, Frank.
And death.
But we're getting closer.
Some day we'll have the same address.
If you see me, wink.

SUMMER PROGRAM

In Ithaca, New York, I dreamed one night
about a Puerto Rican boy
in our summer program
of twenty-two high school juniors.
I was masturbating him.
Waking, I groaned.
Steep hills, lush maples,
ivy–covered brick, and finger lake
couldn't assuage my grim discovery.
It didn't help that my roommate Tom,
straight, described his best friend's
gay escapades back home in Ohio.
Or that I loved Enser's smooth chest,
glimpsed each night in the bathroom.
We studied Hobbes, Locke,
Hume, John Stuart Mill,
while I pursued my independent study
in loneliness and shame.

NEW YORK CITY, 1962

Certain I had epilepsy like Dostoyevsky
and hiding my sexuality like a disease,
I paced Broadway lost in *Life Studies*
as cars avoided my unconscious feet.
I'd never be a poet.
Lusting after Kenny Laptook,
I thought cute boys superior, lucky.
High school was a trial by ordeal.
I decided I detested my father,
whose big belly and monomaniacal ideas
loomed over me like a mountain,
and I believed he and my miserable mother
could read my most intimate thoughts.
Daddy, daddy, you bastard, I'm through.
Plath had one year to live,
Jarrell three, Berryman a whole ten.
I bought *Ariel* and *Homage to Mistress Bradstreet*
in the Paperback Forum across from Columbia,
where whiffs of Ginsberg still scented the air,
but was terrified to enter the West End Bar,
where real poets drank and fought.
Kennedy eyeballed Khrushchev and didn't blink,
but each night I dreamed of the Bomb,
then woke to find reality a nightmare.
It didn't help that late in the year
the famous Dr. Crohn took out my large intestine,

prolific with little growths.
I worried I'd die before I'd written my epic.
Then one day Mr. Berman, my English teacher,
through thick black glasses and a speech impediment,
told me I had talent,
counseling, "Read Yeats, Eliot, Valéry,
Stevens, Apollinaire, Cummings, Frost."
I tried, and limned awkward,
halting lines about the moon and neurons.
I masturbated more than I wrote.
The end of my year was soaked with Hart Crane's
transports
as men's gleaming arms and hips
lit a fevered corner of my brain.
As I walked the dog along Riverside Drive,
young men dressed as women
emerged from behind trees,
calling out, "Hey, young man!"
but I kept walking.
They weren't my type.

ATTENDING A YEATS PLAY
FOR THE FIRST TIME

I can't remember which one it was.
I think Cuchulain was a character—
he who "fought with the invulnerable tide."
Five or six men and women moved
slowly, as in a trance, uttering words
such as a shaman would tell his tribe,
or your grandmother your tiny self afraid of night.
What I remember best was a boy
about my own age, eighteen,
whom some indefinable glow haloed.
Was it his strange, stately phrases?
The way he ceremoniously danced?
Or his elfin face, charming in a way
I couldn't put a finger on?
Afterward, I thought of him again and again,
and his magical body became indistinguishable
from the play's poignant poetry.
I realized I'd fallen in love with both.

PARIS

I paid the old crones in black two *sous*
for permission to sit reading Robbe-Grillet
on a green, wrought iron chair
in the Luxembourg Gardens, safe
in his novels' world of frigid jalousies
and vacant people.
Speaking to no one but waiters, I'd gaze at
black-haired, thick-eyebrowed boys,
wondering what touch would be like.
They had charming manners, I noticed,
and gestured animatedly as they spoke.
But one day one of them tried to pick me up
in front of a bakery and,
petrified, I told him I wasn't interested.
Going back and back
to Leonardo's androgynous St. John in the Louvre,
I thought I might find some answer
in his enigmatic eyes.
I wrote poems in a marbled notebook
about boys alone in the world.
All the time I felt wings
darkening, shadowing me.

And yet there were days I'd stride
in sunshine down the Boulevard St.-Michel
exulting in the glint off the gold Sorbonne dome,

the scent of *croque monsieurs*,
the gleaming volumes of Rimbaud in bookstore bins.

THE NAP, 1966

in memory of Constantin Cavafy

I watched him sleep, the Brazilian boy,
umber-skinned, with the even, fine-ridged nose,
sparrow down on his cheeks,
large eyes like summer earth, now closed.
Watched him breathe, the boy
with whom I went on wild bicycle rides
over icy Pennsylvania hills,
was ravished by Wagner and Mahler
in quaint dorm rooms,
declaimed Yeats and Pound out loud
to the glittering creek.
I could look at him undisturbed.
If I woke him with a kiss,
he would rail and scream,
tell me he wasn't like that,
so I sat very quietly,
noticed the relaxed, brown limbs,
the evenly rising and falling chest,
the twitching lips.
And the boy slept,
and the two of us shared the room for hours.

THE LETTER

Your broad-shouldered swagger and nasty remarks
didn't deter me from adoring
your tawny Brazilian skin,
the jet-black arm-hairs highlighted against it,
and the way you'd declaim *Ulysses*
with a little laughing explosion at each turn of wit.
Leaning close to me, you'd tap my knee
to make a point.
We'd swoop like swallows on our bicycles
over Pennsylvania hills into mapled valleys,
our whoops fusing in frigid air,
eyes glistening bright as any russet leaf.
We'd devour beef stew in the college cafeteria,
then down beers and swoon together to *Tannhäuser*.

But after I wrote you formally, explicitly,
placed the letter myself in your narrow brass mailbox,
then found you later crying face down on your bed,
sobbing "I'm not that way,"
I was left holding the limp end of a stick
that you denied was love, and denied and denied,
and still I do not believe you.

DECADE

I arrived on the Coast
during
the Summer of Love,
made the most of it:
gave up poetry,
met Ann,
became a man,
learned loss,
smoked grass,
went mad,
got well,
lay with Lisa,
knew blues,
loved Bob,
loved Paul
(didn't tell
either one),
met Jill,
got wed,
finished school,
left town.

ORLÉANS

Gleaming modern buses circled tarnished, green
"Joanie on Her Pony"
(as the few Americans in town called her).
The Maid of Orléans had been corroding for centuries,
natives assured me.

Young, my wife and I knew little of wear and tear.
I orbited Joanie, too, high on lemon tea
sipped at the high-ceilinged, chandeliered Café de la
Chancellerie,
where the bow-tied waiter always placed service on the
table with a flourish.
Marigolds and zinnias perfumed Joanie's feet
like bouquets piled up for a bride.
Cream puffs, raspberry tarts, and chocolate
"porcupines" welcomed us
to the bakery Au Petit Duc as did its plump, proper
women clerks
with their musical *Bonjour, Monsieurdame's*.
The main cathedral resembled a festive wedding cake
with its two lacy, ornamented towers.

Summer morphed into fall,
which bent oak branches into the Loiret River,
where they multiplied and lost themselves.
Children went back to school,

briefcases hanging from their backs.
I began teaching *American Poetry* and *The Modern American Novel*
at the university.
Pheasant made its appearance in the *boucheries*,
trussed and headless.

With the snow, the pink roses of the outskirts disappeared,
and the Orléannais retreated into their elegant apartments,
except to go shopping for leeks, mandarins, and veal *escalopes*.
Jill and I savored each scenic bus ride to the university,
each ordinary conversation with the Legrands next door,
knowing my fellowship would end after spring.

In April, lupine bloomed in the Forêt d'Orléans
and mistletoe hung precariously from the branches.
May brought the Joan of Arc parade
with its young woman chosen to ride a white horse
through town.
In June, we sold the furniture to the next resident.
The apartment looked smaller empty.

Now, years later,
I think about the way the woman from the post office

waved to us as she marched in the parade,
about shoppers squeezing the Camemberts,
and TV soccer game announcers calling the best players
des stars.
And people must still be filling the bakeries for early
bread,
gossiping over strong coffee in the cafés,
and circling Joanie on their mopeds,
who's become even a little more tarnished,
a little older.

IN THE OLD CITY

Sitting in my California living room,
I wonder if an American Jew sporting a red tee shirt
that spells out *Coca-Cola* in Hebrew
can still nose around the covered passageways
of the Arab Quarter as I did,
chat with a trinket vendor,
savor a flat, white-and-orange pastry in a dim bakery,
sink deeper and deeper into ancient stone,
velvet tapestry, and musky spice
until the soul of the place becomes his soul.

In 1978, when Sadat and Begin
clasped hands in the Rose Garden,
hope was as perceptible as the drifting incense in Old
City air,
and my friends and I greeted one another daily in the
pottery shop
full of hand-decorated cups, trays, tiles,
in the café where old men sat drinking potent, sweet
coffee,
at the dried fruit stall piled with apricots, figs, dates.

But one day that year the merchants suddenly
shut the metal canopies of their shops and fled
as a group of teenagers stormed down an alley
shouting "Palestine, Palestine!"

chased by a squadron of olive-clad soldiers
running at full speed, Uzis bristling.
I pressed my back as flat as possible
against a wall.

Now, twenty-five years later,
I ride BART to my job in San Francisco,
hike on weekends in the East Bay hills,
have no Arab friends.
I dream I can return there,
that the same fabric vendor, café waiter, and spice merchant
will be there to greet me,
to touch the soft flesh of my hand with theirs,
to share dried peaches, *baklava*, Turkish coffee.

CASTRO AND MARKET

in memory of Thom Gunn

I hesitated at the traffic light.
The intersection filled with a flood of men,
leathered, tee-shirted, shaved-headed, sure, in heat.
Poised behind me was a life of books,
the embrace of several tender women.
Ahead of me loomed—I knew not what.
I didn't know it then, but bone and sinew
drove me on, body's truth that roared,
not asking me if I agreed or not.
Life hovered at that intersection,
trembled, looked deep inside,
then opened to the teeming world and,
when the light turned, plunged.

CASTRO DAYS

I miss those sizzling days when *fuck* and *suck*
were the dominant paradigm, when we'd all
gather on Castro Street by windows where
leather, lubricant, poppers, and dildos were displayed
as we displayed ourselves to each other
as throbbing, slick, hard things.
I plunged, lost myself, with Mark, Jim, Tom,
nameless others on spermy mattresses,
in park bushes, on the street.
If each of us could merge with thousands of others,
we'd form a mass bigger than any puny self.

Then I got sick.
I'd never thought anything could kill love.
I shook with fever, ran to the bathroom,
was covered with sores.
By the time I recovered, all our world
was shivering, shrunk, and dying.

Now when I walk the street, it's as an ego,
separate, different, doomed to die.
When my guy and I make love we melt
into each other, then emerge a couple, self and self.
But at night sometimes I think of the days
when all the world seemed to come together,
when death was murdered and everyone in love.

REBORN

Infected:
something I'd done wrong,
a curse,
unlucky adumbration
of my new life of love?
"If you swallow viscous sperm,
your saliva turns to bugs and germs":
sardonic syllogism.
Three months of cock and ass
followed by how many of suffering
before I'd die?
The doctor said, "It's GRID."
February.

I paced the streets of Berkeley
in three sweaters, parka, and scarf,
warmed mainly by self-pity.
March passed, spring
a fevered blur of naps and nights,
summer and fall spent sweating, weak,
gazing at distant men in cafés,
lamenting wasted sunshine.

Then surprise!
Well in January,
"first to recover" from the disease.

Each bare sycamore branch stood out
against the sky.
Had I been meant to live;
was it a test?
Twenty years later, I look back
and enjoy each breath I take.

MEDITERRANEUM CAFFE, BERKELEY

Never did fit in here,
even though I thought I should.
Came and loitered among gnarly drunks,
hot-eyed poets, a hundred varieties of
off-beat castoff and dissenter.
Didn't they recognize me as brother,
me with my hatred of bosses,
my awkwardness,
my poetry?
But shyness isn't a credential
for joining the counterculture,
and I don't know the hardscrabble streets.
My suffering has been highfalutin:
delicate gay slighted by husky men,
artist misunderstood by the starched university . . .
I don't belong here.
Yet I like to sit among the dissatisfied,
the bittersweet anyway:
where else do I belong?

PORTLAND, OREGON
for Arnold and Gloria Suffin

Everything's green on this spring day in Oregon:
overhanging oak branches, license plates, my heart.
The clear sky shelters me
from the rushing darkness of home.
I breathe deep and laugh as though eighteen again,
inhale lavender,
dodge twirling maple seeds,
stumble over sticky chestnuts on the sidewalk.
Traveling six hundred miles has taken me to a different
world
where strangers hail each other on the street,
the air's sweet as a plum,
and it takes minutes to reach the green belt
that ties the city's robe gently closed.
I stroll down a lane where finches and nuthatches sing,
swearing I will live differently from now on.

ARNOLD SUFFIN'S SCULPTURE
BIRD IN FLIGHT

White, flying into myself,
I fold marble wings and tail
for this frigid, solitary voyage I undertake
for you.

Perched in your living room,
I soar in deathless space
on the other side of your world.

Though I understand everything,
I can explain none of it to you
but arch my neck in a curve

that makes you ache
to run your hand along my icy back.

MEDFORD, OREGON

for Nicholas Follansbee and Drew Giambrone

Morning sun burnishes ragged hills of spiky pines
with a golden sheen.
Your log cabin, deep in shaggy woods,
seems a world apart.
We've barbecued juicy burgers,
played with the dogs Auggie, Stella, Blanche,
listened to Mozart and Madonna,
talked half the night.
Since sunrise I've sat here in a rickety wooden rocker,
my feet on straw and chocolate earth,
trees and flowers glowing like lamps,
birds singing their hearts out,
air dancing with gnats and dust.

AT HOME IN A FOREIGN COUNTRY

Lonely and homesick in Vancouver,
I've discovered Maxim's Restaurant—not Parisian,
but of the lineage of Li Po, Tu Fu, Su Tung-P'o.
No poets here, though, just plain folk slurping *fun*,
confiding into cell phones,
savoring the afternoon sweet as lychee custard.
And indeed, my chow mein's satisfying as a whole
family banquet.
I don't know if Wang Wei ate it,
but it makes my pen flow as though writing *shih*.
I relish the old man over there leaning into his noodle
soup,
that family with its two jet-haired, shiny-eyed boys,
the pale man in horn-rimmed glasses who might read
books.
I gaze at the Chinese newspaper I bought on the street,
not being able to read even the headlines.
I scribble five poems in the style of T'ao Ch'ien.
What is it that draws me here?
Did I live in Shanghai in another life?
Was I a court official who wrote delicate, learned
verses?
I sip sweet, milky Hong Kong Style tea for a long time,
at home in Canada.

GIBSON'S LANDING, CANADA

for Gloria Grover

No sidewalks here,
or traffic lights.
Few cars rumble past your cabin.
The phone never stirs.
We get up late,
sip Keemun tea,
discuss Schubert, Isaiah,
death.
Fifty-seven, I muse about
being HIV positive.
Eighty-five, you reflect
on God.
We've been friends
for forty years.
Walking to town,
we gaze at boats that sway slightly
in the curved sickle of the harbor,
the water glowing like milk.
As we slip into the ocean in midafternoon,
its shockingly cold fingers wake me
to jutting pines, violet peaks, drifting logs.
The air's clear as a baby's skin.
Above us a bald eagle plays
with air currents.
Later, we eat chili

while watching firs shift
in silky late sun.
The night is deep and long,
filled with many-colored ships
and glimmering lights.

SWIMMING AT GIBSON'S LANDING

Encircled by violet, pine-covered peaks,
the bay blazes like a shield.
I plunge into icy, clear ripples,
comfortable as a seal,
and drift out to where logs float by
waving flags of loose bark.
The water shocks my skin awake,
chills those mountains far away
as though we formed one body,
touches the trees that plunge roots into wet loam,
clouds piling up their festive cumuli,
smooth stones that press against my feet.
Every muscle in my body sings.
Finally I lie on hot rocks
ready to give myself up
for any old feast,
any celebration at all.

MONDRIAN'S HOUSE

could be built right on this page
using horizontal black lines of stark print
and white spaces dividing word from word,
with a few colorful images thrown in.
Each word in its proper location,
the doorway to the emotions just so.
What do you say to make a house out of a poem?
Do you put yourself in it,
like Mr. Mondrian in one famous photo,
proud, erect,
parallel to his own doorjamb and closet?
Or do you keep yourself out of it,
as in another celebrated shot, and just depict
Mondrian's spare studio with its white walls a
counterpoint
to dark, rectangular wood panels,
Panama hat hanging on peg,
vase of wooden flowers on the table,
and spiraling staircase glimpsed through doorway?
I would say, do whatever you want
as long as you build it clean and strong.
Mr. Mondrian wouldn't want it any other way.
Here are the ceiling beams, here the walls.
I welcome you to the harmonious, simple poem.
When you enter, please be respectful of the artist.
His home is his castle,
so be sure to wipe your shoes on the mat.

NOTES

Art Epiphanies: There is a key scene in *War and Peace* in
which Prince Andrew, severely wounded in a battle
with the French, lies supine and perceives eternity
in the clouds passing above his head (Louise and
Aylmer Maude's translation, New York: Simon and
Schuster, 1942, pages 301-2). Cody's Books is in
Berkeley, California.

Captain Jack's Wharf was a picturesque tourist attraction
during the summers I spent in Provincetown,
Massachusetts in the nineteen fifties and sixties.
When I returned to the town around 1995 after
an absence of many years, I came across a post card
of the structure identifying it as an "old Cape Cod
wharf," Captain Jack's name having apparently been
washed off the pier's reputation, as if by the lapping
of the waves.

Leonardo's Tomb at Amboise: Leonardo da Vinci is buried
in a tiny chapel on the grounds of the Château of
Amboise in the Loire Valley. His home, Clos-Lucé,
is a couple of hundred yards away.

Ruby King Chinese Bakery is in the Chinatown of
Oakland, California.

The 49 Van Ness Bus route is in San Francisco.

How We Were Alike, Jimmy: The lines on the middle
of page 35 are quoted from Schuyler's poem
"Suddenly," and the final four lines on page 36

from his poem "Six something."

Baseball: Tom Tresh played center field for the Yankees for several of the nineteen-sixties.

Grayness: The Rose Garden referred to is the one in Berkeley. Tilden Park borders on Berkeley and Kensington.

A Brief Study of Beverages: This poem is dedicated to the memory of Kenneth Koch because written in the style of his poems in *The Art of Love*. Note that Koch pronounced his name "Coke".

Frank O'Hara's Book Jackson Pollock: O'Hara was not only a great poet but an art critic and special assistant and then curator at the Museum of Modern Art in New York during the fifties and sixties.

Reborn: "GRID," or "Gay Related Immunodeficiency Disease," was for a short time the name for what came to known as AIDS.

Mediterraneum Caffe, Berkeley: The "Med" Café, situated on Telegraph Avenue in Berkeley, is the oldest café in Berkeley, having first opened in 1958.

Arnold Suffin's Bird in Flight: Suffin is a remarkable sculptor and painter who lives and works in Portland, Oregon and deserves to be better known. I'm lucky enough to own this white sculpture carved out of marble quarried in Pietrasanta, Italy.

Gibson's Landing, Canada is a small seaside village on the Sunshine Coast of British Columbia, a half hour's dramatic ferry ride from Vancouver.

Mondrian's House: Arnold Newman's 1942 photograph of Mondrian standing in his studio at 353 East 56th Street in New York City is remarkable in that it shows the artist standing very erect in his black suit, his tall, elegant figure and long, angular face blending into the lines of the studio and of the largely black-and-white, vertical-and-horizontal-lined paintings around him. André Kertesz produced a famous photograph in 1926, *"Chez Mondrian,"* that depicts the entrance to Mondrian's Paris studio in which everything except doormat and Panama hat is made of wood—even the flowers in the vase.

ABOUT THE AUTHOR

Marc Elihu Hofstadter was born in New York City in 1945. He received his B.A. degree from Swarthmore College in 1967, and his Ph.D. in Literature from the University of California at Santa Cruz in 1975. From 1977 to 1978 he was Fulbright Lecturer in American Literature at the Université d'Orléans, and in 1978 and 1979 he taught American literature at Tel Aviv University. In 1980 he obtained his M.L.S. degree from the University of California at Berkeley and, from 1982 to 2005, served as the librarian of the City of San Francisco's transit agency. He has published two volumes of poetry, *House of Peace* (Mother's Hen Press) and *Visions* (Scarlet Tanager Press), and his poems, translations, and essays have appeared in many magazines and in the anthology of writings about tea, *Steeped*. Hofstadter is a member of one of the United States' leading intellectual families. His uncle Robert Hofstadter won the Nobel Prize in physics, his cousins Douglas and Richard Hofstader were both awarded the Pulitzer Prize, his father Albert was an acclaimed philosopher, his mother Manya Huber an award-winning concert pianist, and his uncle Samuel Huber a noted painter. Hofstadter lives in Walnut Creek, California with his partner, the artist David Zurlin.